MW01029580

The Life of Josiah Henson

An Inspiration for Harriet Beecher Stowe's Uncle Tom

JOSIAH HENSON

DOVER PUBLICATIONS, INC.
Mineola, New York

DOVER THRIFT EDITIONS

GENERAL EDITOR: MARY CAROLYN WALDREP
EDITOR OF THIS VOLUME: JIM MILLER

Bibliographical Note

This Dover edition, first published in 2015, is an unabridged republication of *The Life of Josiah Henson Formerly a Slave, Now an inhabitant of Canada, as Narrated by Himself*, originally published in 1849 by Arthur D. Phelps, Boston.

Library of Congress Cataloging-in-Publication Data

Henson, Josiah, 1789–1883, author.
    The life of Josiah Henson : an inspiration for Harriet Beecher Stowe's Uncle Tom / Josiah Henson. — Dover edition.
       p. cm.
    Original edition published: Boston : A. D. Phelps, 1849.
    Original edition has subtitle: formerly a slave, now an inhabitant of Canada.
    ISBN-13: 978-0-486-80045-5
    ISBN-10: 0-486-80045-8
    1. Henson, Josiah, 1789–1883. 2. Slaves—United States—Biography. 3. African Americans—Biography. 4. Fugitive slaves—United States—Biography. 5. Fugitive slaves—Canada—Biography. 6. Blacks—Canada—Biography. 7. Clergy—Canada—Biography. I. Title.

E444.H52 2015
306.3'62092—dc23

2015028084

Manufactured in the United States by RR Donnelley
80045801   2015
www.doverpublications.com

Advertisement

The following memoir was written from the dictation of Josiah Henson. A portion of the story was told, which, when written, was read to him, that any errors of statement might be corrected. The substance of it, therefore, the facts, the reflections, and very often the words, are his; and little more than the structure of the sentences belongs to another.

The narrative, in this form, necessarily loses the attraction derived from the earnest manner, the natural eloquence of a man who tells a story in which he is deeply interested; but it is hoped that enough remains to repay perusal, and that the character of the man, and the striking nature of the events of his life will be thought to justify the endeavor to make them more extensively known. The story has this advantage, that it is not fiction, but fact; and it will be found fruitful in instruction by those who attentively consider its lessons.

LIFE OF JOSIAH HENSON

I was born, June 15, 1789, in Charles County, Maryland, on a farm belonging to Mr. Francis N., about a mile from Port Tobacco. My mother was the property of Dr. Josiah McP., but was hired by Mr. N., to whom my father belonged. The only incident I can remember, which occurred while my mother continued on N.'s farm, was the appearance of my father one day, with his head bloody and his back lacerated. He was in a state of great excitement, and though it was all a mystery to me at the age of three or four years, it was explained at a later period, and I understood that he had been suffering the cruel penalty of the Maryland law for beating a white man. His right ear had been cut off close to his head, and he had received a hundred lashes on his back. He had beaten the overseer for a brutal assault on my mother, and this was his punishment. Furious at such treatment, my father became a different man, and was so morose, disobedient and intractable, that Mr. N. determined to sell him. He accordingly parted with him, not long after, to his son, who lived in Alabama; and neither my mother nor I, ever heard of him again. He was naturally, as I understood afterwards from my mother and other persons, a man of amiable temper, and of considerable energy of character; but it is not strange that he should be essentially changed by such cruelty and injustice under the sanction of law.

After the sale of my father by N., and his leaving Maryland for Alabama, Dr. McP. would no longer hire out my mother to N. She returned, therefore, to the estate of the doctor, who was very much kinder to his slaves than the generality of planters, never suffering them to be struck by any one. He was, indeed, a man of good natural impulses, kind-hearted, liberal, and jovial. The latter quality was so much developed as to be his great failing; and though his convivial excesses were not thought of as a fault by the community in which he lived, and did not even prevent his having a high reputation for goodness of heart, and an almost saintlike benevolence, yet they were, nevertheless, his ruin. My mother, and her young family of three girls and three boys, of which I was the youngest, resided on this estate for two or three years, during which my only recollections are of being rather a pet of the doctor's, who thought I was a bright child, and of being much impressed with what I afterwards recognized as the deep piety and devotional feeling and habits of my mother. I do not know how, or where she acquired her knowledge of God, or her acquaintance with the Lord's prayer, which she so frequently repeated and taught me to repeat. I remember seeing her often on her knees endeavoring to arrange her thoughts in prayers appropriate to her situation, but which amounted to little more than constant ejaculation, and the repetition of short phrases, which were within my infant comprehension, and have remained in my memory to this hour.

After this brief period of comparative comfort, however, the death of Dr. McP. brought about a revolution in our condition, which common as such things are in slave countries, can never be imagined by those not subject to them, nor recollected by those who have been, without emotions of grief and indignation deep and ineffaceable. The doctor was riding from one of his scenes of riotous excess, when, falling from his horse, in crossing a little run, not a foot deep, he was unable to save himself from drowning.

In consequence of his decease it became necessary to sell the estate and the slaves, in order to divide up the property among the heirs; and we were all put up at auction and sold to the highest bidder, and scattered over various parts of the country. My brothers and sisters were bid off one by one, while my mother, holding my hand, looked on in an agony of grief, the cause of which I but ill understood at first, but which dawned on my mind, with dreadful clearness, as the sale proceeded. My mother was then separated from me, and put up in her turn. She was bought by a man named Isaac R., residing in Montgomery county, and then I was offered to the assembled purchasers. My mother, half distracted with the parting forever from all her children, pushed through the crowd, while the bidding for me was going on, to the spot where R. was standing. She fell at his feet, and clung to his knees, entreating him in tones that a mother only could command, to buy her baby as well as herself, and spare to her one of her little ones at least. Will it, can it be believed that this man, thus appealed to, was capable not merely of turning a deaf ear to her supplication, but of disengaging himself from her with such violent blows and kicks, as to reduce her to the necessity of creeping out of his reach, and mingling the groan of bodily suffering with the sob of a breaking heart? Yet this was one of my earliest observations of men; an experience which has been common to me with thousands of my race, the bitterness of which its frequency cannot diminish to any individual who suffers it, while it is dark enough to overshadow the whole after-life with something blacker than a funeral pall. I was bought by a stranger. Almost immediately, however, whether my childish strength, at five or six years of age, was overmastered by such scenes and experience, or from some accidental cause, I fell sick, and seemed to my new master so little likely to recover, that he proposed to R., the purchaser of my mother, to take me too at such a trifling rate that it could not be refused. I was thus providentially restored to my mother; and under her care, destitute as she was of the proper means of nursing me, I recovered my health, and grew up to be an uncommonly vigorous and healthy boy and man.

The character of R., the master whom I faithfully served for many years, is by no means an uncommon one in any part of the world; but it is to be regretted that a domestic institution should anywhere put it in the power of such a one to tyrannize over his fellow beings, and inflict so much needless misery as is sure to be produced by such a man in such a position. Coarse and vulgar in his habits, unprincipled and cruel in his general deportment, and especially addicted to the vice of licentiousness, his slaves had little opportunity for relaxation from wearying labor, were supplied with the scantiest means of sustaining their toil by necessary food and had no security for personal rights. The natural tendency of slavery is, to convert the master into a tyrant, and the slave into the cringing, treacherous, false, and thieving victim of tyranny. R. and his slaves were no exception to the general rule, but might be cited as apt illustrations of the nature of the case.

My earliest employments were, to carry buckets of water to the men at work, to hold a horseplow, used for weeding between the rows of corn, and as I grew older and taller, to take care of master's saddle-horse. Then a hoe was put into my hands, and I was soon required to do the day's work of a man; and it was not long before I could do it, at least as well as my associates in misery.

The every-day life of a slave on one of our southern plantations, however frequently it may have been described, is generally little known at the North; and must be mentioned as a necessary illustration of the character and habits of the slave and the slave-holder, created and perpetuated by their relative position. The principal food of those upon my master's plantation consisted of corn meal, and salt herrings; to which was added in summer a little buttermilk, and the few vegetables which each might raise for himself and his family, on the little piece of ground which was assigned to him for the purpose, called a truck patch. The meals were two, daily. The first, or breakfast, was taken at 12 o'clock, after laboring from daylight; and the other when the work of the remainder of the day was over. The only dress was of tow cloth, which for the young, and often even for those who had passed the period of childhood, consisted of a single garment, something like a shirt, but longer, reaching to the ankles; and for the older, a pair of pantaloons, or a gown, according to the sex; while some kind of round jacket, or overcoat, might be added in winter, a wool hat once in two or three years, for the males, and a pair of coarse shoes once a year. Our lodging was in log huts, of a single small room, with no other floor than the trodden earth, in which ten or a dozen persons—men, women, and children—might sleep, but which could not protect them from dampness and cold, nor permit the existence of the common decencies of life. There were neither beds, nor furniture of any description—a blanket being the only addition to the dress of the day for protection from the chillness of the air or the earth. In these hovels were we penned at night, and fed by day; here were the children born, and the sick—neglected. Such were the provisions for the daily toil of the slave.

Notwithstanding this system of management, however, I grew to be a robust and vigorous lad, and at fifteen years of age, there were few who could compete with me in work, or in sport—for not even the condition of a slave can altogether repress the animal spirits of the young negro. I was competent to all the work that was done upon the farm, and could run faster and farther, wrestle longer, and jump higher, than anybody about me. My master and my fellow slaves used to look upon me, and speak of me, as a wonderfully smart fellow, and prophesy the great things I should do when I became a man. A casual word of this sort, sometimes overheard, would fill me with a pride and ambition which some would think impossible in a negro slave, degraded, starved, and abused as I was, and had been from my earliest recollection. But the love of superiority is not confined to kings and emperors; and it is a positive fact, that pride and ambition were as active in my soul as probably they ever were in that of the greatest soldier or statesman. The objects I pursued, I must admit, were not just the same as theirs. Mine to be first in the field, whether we were hoeing, mowing or reaping; to surpass those of my own age, or indeed any age, in athletic exercises; and to obtain, if possible, the favorable regard of the petty despot who ruled over us. This last was an exercise of the understanding, rather than of the affections; and I was guided in it more by what I supposed would be effectual, than by a nice judgment of the propriety of the means I used.

I obtained great influence with my companions, as well by the superiority I showed in labor and in sport, as by the assistance I yielded them, and the favor I conferred upon them, from impulses which I cannot consider as wrong, though it was necessary for me to conceal sometimes the act as well as its motive. I have toiled and induced others to toil, many an extra hour, in order to show my master what an excellent day's work had been accomplished, and to win a kind word or a benevolent deed from his callous heart. In general, indifference, or a cool calculation of my value to him, were my reward, chilling those hopes of an improvement in my condition, which was the ultimate object of my efforts. I was much more easily moved to compassion and sympathy than he was; and one of the means I took to gain the good-will of my fellow sufferers, was by taking from him some things he did not give, in part payment of my extra labor. The condition of the male slave is bad enough, Heaven knows; but that of the female, compelled to perform unfit labor, sick, suffering and bearing the burdens of her own sex unpitied and unaided, as well as the toils which belong to the other, has often oppressed me with a load of sympathy. And sometimes, when I have seen them starved, and miserable, and unable to help themselves, I have helped them to some of the comforts which they were denied by him who owned them, and which my companions had not the wit or the daring to procure. Meat was not a part of our regular food; but my master had plenty of sheep and pigs, and sometimes I have picked out the best one I could find in the flock, or the drove, carried it a mile or two into the woods, slaughtered it, cut it up, and distributed it among the poor creatures, to whom it was at once food, luxury, and medicine. Was this wrong? I can only say that, at this distance of time, my conscience does not reproach me for it, and that then I esteemed it among the best of my deeds.

By means of the influence thus acquired, the increased amount of work done upon the farm, and by the detection of the knavery of the overseer, who plundered his employer for more selfish ends, and through my watchfulness was caught in the act and dismissed, I was promoted to be superintendent of the farm work, and managed to raise more than double the crops, with more cheerful and willing labor, than was ever seen on the estate before.

Previous to my attaining this important station, however, an incident occurred of so powerful an influence on my intellectual development, my prospect of improvement in character, as well as condition, my chance of religious culture, and in short, on my whole nature, body and soul, that it deserves especial notice and commemoration. There was a person living at Georgetown, a few miles only from R.'s Plantation, whose business was that of a baker, and whose character was that of an upright, benevolent, Christian man. He was noted especially for his detestation of slavery, and his resolute avoidance of the employment of slave labor in his business. He would not even hire a slave, the price of whose toil must be paid to his master, but contented himself with the work of his own hands, and with such free labor as he could procure. His reputation was high, not only for this almost singular abstinence from what no one about him thought wrong, but for his general probity and excellence. This man occasionally served as a minister of the Gospel, and preached in a neighborhood where preachers were somewhat rare at that period. One Sunday when he was to officiate in this way, at a place three or four miles distant, my mother persuaded me to ask master's leave to go and hear him; and although such permission was not given freely or often, yet his favor to me was shown for this once by allowing me to go, without much scolding, but not without a pretty distinct intimation of what would befall me, if I did not return immediately after the close of the service. I hurried off, pleased with the opportunity, but without any definite expectations of benefit or amusement; for up to this period of my life, and I was then eighteen years old, I had never heard a sermon, nor any discourse or conversation whatever, upon religious topics, except what had been impressed upon me by my mother, of the responsibility of all to a Supreme Being. When I arrived at the place of meeting, the services were so far advanced that the speaker was just beginning his discourse, from the text, Hebrews ii. 9; "That he, by the grace of God, should taste of death for every man." This was the first text of the Bible to which I had ever listened, knowing it to be such. I have never forgotten it, and scarce a day has passed since, in which I have not recalled it, and the sermon that was preached from it. The divine character of

Jesus Christ, his life and teachings, his sacrifice of himself for others, his death and resurrection were all alluded to, and some of the points were dwelt upon with great power,—great, at least, to me, who heard of these things for the first time in my life. I was wonderfully impressed, too with the use which the preacher made of the last words of the text, "for every man." He said the death of Christ was not designed for the benefit of a select few only, but for the salvation of the world, for the bond as well as the free; and he dwelt on the glad tidings of the Gospel to the poor, the persecuted, and the distressed, its deliverance to the captive, and the liberty wherewith Christ has made us free, till my heart burned within me, and I was in a state of the greatest excitement at the thought that such a being as Jesus Christ had been described should have died for me—for me among the rest, a poor, despised, abused slave, who was thought by his fellow creatures fit for nothing but unrequited toil, and ignorance, for mental and bodily degradation. I immediately determined to find out something more about "Christ and him crucified;" and revolving the things which I had heard in my mind as I went home, I became so excited that I turned aside from the road into the woods, and prayed to God for light and for aid with an earnestness, which, however unenlightened, was at least sincere and heartfelt; and which the subsequent course of my life has led me to imagine might not have been unacceptable to Him who heareth prayer. At all events, I date my conversion, and my awakening to a new life—to a consciousness of superior powers and destiny to any thing I had before conceived of—from this day, so memorable to me. I used every means and opportunity of inquiry into religious matters; and so deep was my conviction of their superior importance to every thing else, so clear my perception of my own faults, and so undoubting my observation of the sin and darkness that surrounded me, that I could not help talking much on these subjects with those about me; and it was not long before I began to pray with them, and exhort them, and to impart to the poor slaves those little glimmerings of light from another world, which had reached my own eye. In a few years I became quite an esteemed preacher among them, and I will not believe it is vanity which leads me to think I was useful to some.

I must return, however, for the present, to the course of my life in secular affairs, the facts of which it is my principal object to relate. The difference between the manner in which it was designed that all men should regard one another, as children of the same Father, and the manner in which men actually do treat each other, as if they were placed here for mutual annoyance and destruction, is well exemplified by an incident that happened to me within a year or two from this period, that is, when I was nineteen or twenty years old. My master's habits were such as were common enough among the dissipated planters of the neighborhood; and one of their frequent practices was, to assemble on Saturday or Sunday, which were their holidays, and gamble, run horses, or fight gamecocks, discuss politics, and drink whiskey, and brandy and water, all day long. Perfectly aware that they would not be able to find their own way home at night, each one ordered a slave, his particular attendant, to come after him and help him home. I was chosen for this confidential duty by my master; and many is the time I have held him on his horse, when he could not hold himself in the saddle, and walked by his side in darkness and mud from the tavern to his house. Of course, quarrels and brawls of the most violent description were frequent consequences of these meetings, and whenever they became especially dangerous, and glasses were thrown, dirks drawn, and pistols fired, it was the duty of the slaves, to rush in, and each one was to drag his master from the fight, and carry him home. To tell the truth, this was a part of my business for which I felt no reluctance. I was young, remarkably athletic and self-relying, and in such affrays I carried it with a high hand, and would elbow my way among the whites, whom it would have been almost death for me to strike, seize my master and drag him out, mount him on his horse, or crowd him into his buggy, with the ease with which I would handle a bag of corn, and at the same time with the pride of conscious superiority, and the kindness inspired by performing an act of benevolence. I knew I was doing for him what he could not do for himself, and showing my superiority to others, and acquiring their respect in some degree, at the same time.

On one of these occasions, my master got into a quarrel with his brother's overseer, who was one of the party, and in rescuing the former, I suppose I was a little more rough with the latter than usual. I remember his falling upon the floor, and very likely it was from the effects of a push from me, or a movement of my elbow. He attributed his fall to me, rather than to the whiskey he had drunk, and treasured up his vengeance for the first favorable opportunity. About a week afterwards, I was sent by my master to a place a few miles distant, on horseback, with some letters. I took a short cut through a lane, separated by gates from the high road, and bounded by a fence on each side. This lane passed through some of the farm owned by my master's brother, and his overseer was in the adjoining field, with three negroes, when I went by. On my return, a half an hour afterwards, the overseer was sitting on the fence; but I could see nothing of the black fellows. I rode on, utterly unsuspicious of any trouble, but as I approached, he jumped off the fence, and at the same moment two of the negroes sprung up from under the bushes, where they had been concealed, and stood with him, immediately in front of me; while the third sprang over the fence just behind me. I was thus enclosed between what I could no longer doubt were hostile forces. The overseer seized my horse's bridle, and ordered me to alight, in the usual elegant phraseology used by such men to slaves. I asked what I was to alight for. "To take the cursedest flogging you ever had in your life, you d—d black scoundrel." "But what am I to be flogged for, Mr. L.," I asked. "Not a word" said he, "but 'light at once, and take off your jacket." I saw there was nothing else to be done, and slipped off the horse on the opposite side from him. "Now take off your shirt," cried he; and as I demurred at this, he lifted a stick he had in his hand to strike me, but so suddenly and violently, that he frightened the horse, which broke away from him and ran home. I was thus left without means of escape, to sustain the attacks of four men, as well as I might. In avoiding Mr. L.'s blow, I had accidentally got into a corner of the fence, where I could not be approached except in front. The overseer called upon the negroes to seize me; but they, knowing something of my physical power, were rather slow to obey. At length they did their best, and as they brought themselves within my reach, I knocked them down successively; and one of them trying to trip up my feet when he was down, I gave him a kick with my heavy shoe, which knocked out several of his front teeth, and sent him groaning away. Meanwhile, the cowardly overseer was availing himself of every opportunity to hit me over the head with his stick, which was not heavy enough to knock me down, though it drew blood freely. At length, tired of the length of the affray, he seized a stake, six or seven feet long, from the fence, and struck at me with his whole strength. In attempting to ward off the blow, my right arm was broken, and I was brought to the ground; where repeated blows broke both my shoulder blades, and made the blood gush from my mouth copiously. The two blacks begged him not to murder me, and he just left me as I was, telling me to learn what it was to strike a white man. The alarm had been raised at the house, by seeing the horse come back without his rider, and it was not long before assistance arrived to convey me home. It may be supposed it was not done without some suffering on my part; as, besides my broken arm and the wounds on my head, I could feel and hear the pieces of my shoulder-blades grate against each other with every breath. No physician or surgeon was called to

dress my wounds, and I never knew one to
be called to a slave upon R.'s estate, on any
occasion whatever, and have no knowledge
of such a thing being done on any estate in
the neighborhood. I was attended, if it may
be called attendance, by my master's sister,
who had some reputation in such affairs;
and she splintered up my arm, and bound
up my back as well as she knew how, and
nature did the rest. It was five months
before I could work at all, and the first time
I tried to plough, a hard knock of the coul-
ter against a stone, shattered my shoulder-
blades again, and gave me even greater
agony than at first. I have been unable to
raise my hands to my head from that day to
this. My master prosecuted Mr. L. for
abusing and maiming his slave; and when
the case was tried before the magistrate, he
made a statement of the facts as I have here
related them. When Mr. L. was called upon
to say why he should not be fined for the
offence, he simply stated, without being
put on oath, that he had acted in self-
defence; that I had assaulted him; and that
nothing had saved him from being killed
on the spot by so stout a fellow, but the for-
tunate circumstance that his three negroes
were within call. The result was, that my

master paid all the costs of court. He had the satisfaction of calling Mr. L. a liar and scoundrel, and, afterwards, of beating him in a very thorough manner, for which he had also to pay a fine and costs.

My situation, as overseer, I retained, together with the especial favor of my master, who was not displeased either with saving the expense of a large salary for a white superintendent, or with the superior crops I was able to raise for him. I will not deny that I used his property more freely than he would have done himself, in supplying his people with better food; but if I cheated him in this way, in small matters, it was unequivocally for his own benefit in more important ones; and I accounted, with the strictest honesty, for every dollar I received in the sale of the property entrusted to me. Gradually the disposal of everything raised on the farm, the wheat, oats, hay, fruit, butter, and whatever else there might be, was confided to me, as it was quite evident that I could, and did sell for better prices than any one else he could employ, and he was quite incompetent to attend to the business himself. For many years I was his factotum, and supplied him with all his means for all his purposes, whether they were good or bad. I had no reason to think highly of his moral character, but it was my duty to be faithful to him, in the position in which he placed me; and I can boldly declare, before God and man, that I was so. I forgave him the causeless blows and injuries he had inflicted on me in childhood and youth, and was proud of the favor he now showed me, and of the character and reputation I had earned by strenuous and persevering efforts.

When I was about twenty-two years of age, I married a very efficient, and, for a slave, a very well-taught girl, belonging to a neighboring family, reputed to be pious and kind, whom I first met at the chapel I attended; and during nearly forty years that have since elapsed, I have had no reason to regret the connection, but many, to rejoice in it, and be grateful for it. She has borne me twelve children, eight of whom survive, and promise to be the comfort of my declining years.

Things remained in this condition for a considerable period; my occupations being to superintend the farming operations, and to sell the produce in the neighboring markets of Washington and Georgetown. Many respectable people, yet living there, may possibly have some recollection of "'Siah," or

"Si," (as they used to call me,) as their market-man; but if they have forgotten me, I remember them with all honest satisfaction.

After passing his youth in the manner I have mentioned in a general way, and which I do not wish more particularly to describe, my master, at the age of forty-five, or upwards, married a young woman of eighteen, who had some little property, and more thrift. Her economy was remarkable, and was certainly no addition to the comfort of the establishment. She had a younger brother, Francis, to whom R. was appointed guardian, and who used to complain—not without reason, I am confident—of the meanness of the provision made for the household; and he would often come to me, with tears in his eyes, to tell me he could not get enough to eat. I made him my friend for life, by sympathizing in his emotions, and satisfying his appetite, sharing with him the food I took care to provide for my own family.

After a time, however, continual dissipation was more than a match for domestic saving. My master fell into difficulty, and from difficulty into a lawsuit with a brother-in-law, who charged him with dishonest management of property confided

to him in trust. The lawsuit was protracted
enough to cause his ruin, of itself. He used
every resource to stave off the inevitable
result, but at length saw no means of relief
but removal to another State. He often
came to my cabin to pass the evening in
lamentations over his misfortune, in curs-
ing his brother-in-law, and asking my
advice and assistance. The first time he ever
intimated to me his ultimate project, he
said he was ruined, that every thing was
gone, that there was but one resource, and
that depended upon me. "How can that be,
master?" said I, in astonishment. Before he
would explain himself, however, he begged
me to promise to do what he should pro-
pose, well knowing, from his past experience, of my character, that I should hold
myself bound by such promise to do all
that it implied, if it were within the limits
of possibility. Solicited in this way, with
urgency and tears, by the man whom I had
so zealously served for twenty years, and
who now seemed absolutely dependent
upon his slave,—impelled, too, by the fear
which he skilfully awakened, that the sher-
iff would seize every one who belonged to
him, and that all would be separated, or
perhaps sold to go to Georgia, or

Louisiana—an object of perpetual dread to
the slave of the more northern States—I
consented, and promised to do all I could
to save him from the fate impending over
him. He then told me I must take his slaves
to his brother, in Kentucky. In vain I repre-
sented to him that I had never travelled a
day's journey from his plantation, and
knew nothing of the way, or the means of
getting to Kentucky. He insisted that such a
smart fellow as I could travel anywhere, he
promised to give me all necessary instructions, and urged that this was the only
course by which he could be saved. The
result was, that I agreed to undertake the
enterprise—certainly no light one for me,
as it could scarcely be considered for even
an experienced manager. There were eighteen negroes, besides my wife, two children,
and myself, to transport nearly a thousand
miles, through a country I knew nothing
about, and in winter time, for we started in
the month of February, 1825. My master
proposed to follow me in a few months,
and establish himself in Kentucky. He furnished me with a small sum of money, and
some provisions; and I bought a one-horse
wagon, to carry them, and to give the
women and children a lift now and then,

and the rest of us were to trudge on foot. Fortunately for the success of the undertaking, these people had been long under my direction, and were devotedly attached to me for the many alleviations I had afforded to their miserable condition, the comforts I had procured them, and the consideration which I had always manifested for them.

Under these circumstances no difficulty arose from want of submission to my authority, and none of any sort, except that which I necessarily encountered from my ignorance of the country, and my inexperience in such business. On arriving at Wheeling, I sold the horse and wagon, and purchased a boat of sufficient size, and floated down the river without further trouble or fatigue, stopping every night to encamp.

I said I had no further trouble, but there was one source of anxiety which I was compelled to encounter, and a temptation I had to resist, the strength of which others can appreciate as well as myself. In passing along the State of Ohio, we were frequently told that we were free, if we chose to be so. At Cincinnati, especially, the coloured people gathered round us and urged us

with much importunity to remain with
them; told us it was folly to go on; and in
short used all the arguments now so famil-
iar to induce slaves to quit their masters.
My companions probably had little perception of the nature of the boon that was
offered to them, and they were willing to
do just as I told them, without a wish to
judge for themselves. Not so with me.
From my earliest recollection, freedom had
been the object of my ambition, a constant
motive to exertion, an ever-present stimu-
lus to gain and save. No other means of
obtaining it, however, had occurred to me,
but purchasing myself of my master. The
idea of running away was not one that I
had ever indulged. I had a sentiment of
honor on the subject, or what I thought
such, which I would not have violated even
for freedom; and every cent which I had
ever felt entitled to call my own, had been
treasured up for this great purpose, till I
had accumulated between thirty and forty
dollars. Now was offered to me an opportunity I had not anticipated. I might liber-
ate my family, my companions, and myself,
without the smallest risk, and without
injustice to any individual, except one
whom we had none of us any reason to

love, who had been guilty of cruelty and
oppression to us all for many years, and
who had never shown the smallest symp-
tom of sympathy with us, or with any one
in our condition. But I need not make the
exception. There would have been no injustice to R. himself—it would have been a
retribution which might be called right-
eous—if I had availed myself of the opportunity thus thrust suddenly upon me.

But it was a punishment which it was
not for me to inflict. I had promised that
man to take his property to Kentucky, and
deposit it with his brother; and this, and
this only, I resolved to do. I left Cincinnati
before night, though I had intended to
remain there, and encamped with my entire
party a few miles below the city. What
advantages I may have lost, by thus throw-
ing away an opportunity of obtaining freedom, I know not; but the perception of my
own strength of character, the feeling of
integrity, the sentiment of high honor, I
have experienced,—these advantages I do
know, and prize; and would not lose them,
nor the recollection of having attained
them, for all that I can imagine to have
resulted from an earlier release from
bondage. I have often had painful doubts

as to the propriety of my carrying so many other individuals into slavery again, and my consoling reflection has been, that I acted as I thought at the time was best.

I arrived at Daviess county, Kentucky, about the middle of April, 1825, and delivered myself and my companions to Mr. Amos R., the brother of my owner, who had a large plantation, with from eighty to one hundred negroes. His house was situated about five miles south of the Ohio River, and fifteen miles above the Yellow Banks, on Big Blackford's Creek. There I remained three years, expecting my master to follow; and employed meantime on the farm, of which I had the general management, in consequence of the recommendation for ability and honesty which I brought with me from Maryland. The situation was in many respects more comfortable than that I had left. The farm was larger, and more fertile, and there was a greater abundance of food, which is, of course, one of the principal sources of the comfort of a slave, debarred, as he is, from so many enjoyments which other men can obtain. Sufficiency of food is a pretty important item in any man's account of life; but is tenfold more so in that of a slave, whose appetite is always stimulated by as much labor as he can perform, and whose mind is little occupied by thought on subjects of deeper interest. My post of superintendent gave me some advantages, too, of which I did not fail to avail myself, particularly with regard to those religious privileges, which, since I first heard of Christ and Christianity, had greatly occupied my mind. In Kentucky, the opportunities of attending on the preaching of whites, as well as blacks, were more numerous; and partly by attending them, and the camp-meetings which occurred from time to time, and partly from studying carefully my own heart, and observing the developments of character around me, in all the stations of life which I could watch, I became better acquainted with those religious feelings which are deeply implanted in the breast of every human being, and learned by practice how best to arouse them, and keep them excited, how to stir up the callous and indifferent, and in general to produce some good religious impressions on the ignorant and thoughtless community by which I was surrounded.

No great amount of theological knowledge is requisite for the purpose. If it had been, it is manifest enough that preaching never could have been my vocation; but I am persuaded that, speaking from the fulness of a heart deeply impressed with its own sinfulness and imperfection, and with the mercy of God, in Christ Jesus, my humble ministrations have not been entirely useless to those who have had less opportunity than myself to reflect upon these all-important subjects. It is certain that I could not refrain from the endeavor to do what I saw others doing in this field; and I labored at once to improve myself and those about me in the cultivation of the harvests which ripen only in eternity. I cannot but derive some satisfaction, too, from the proofs I have had that my services have been acceptable to those to whom they have been rendered. In the course of the three years from 1825 to 1828, I availed myself of all the opportunities of improvement which occurred, and was admitted as a preacher by a Conference of the Methodist Episcopal Church.

In the spring of the year 1828, news arrived from my master that he was unable to induce his wife to accompany him to Kentucky, and he must therefore remain where he was. He sent out an agent to sell all his slaves but me and my family, and to carry back the proceeds to him. And now another of those heart-rending scenes was to be witnessed, which had impressed itself so deeply on my childish soul. Husbands and wives, parents and children were to be separated forever. Affections, which are as strong in the African as in the European were to be cruelly disregarded; and the iron selfishness generated by the hateful "institution" was to be exhibited in its most odious and naked deformity. I was exempted from a personal share in the dreadful calamity, but I could not see without the deepest grief the agony which I recollected in my own mother, and which was again brought before my eyes in the persons with whom I had been long associated; nor could I refrain from the bitterest feeling of hatred of the system and those who sustain it. What else, indeed, can be the feeling of the slave, liable at every moment of his life to these frightful and unnecessary calamities, which may be caused by the caprice of the abandoned, or the supposed necessities of the better part of the slaveholders, and inflicted upon him without sympathy or redress, under the sanction of the laws which uphold the institution? I lamented my agency in bringing the poor creatures hither, if such was to be the end of the expedition; but I could not reproach myself with having made their condition really worse, nor with any thing but complying with the commands of a heartless master.

In the course of the summer of 1828, a Methodist preacher, a white man of some reputation, visited our neighborhood, and I became acquainted with him. He was soon interested in me, and visited me frequently, and one day talked to me in a confidential manner about my position. He said I ought to be free; that I had too much capacity to be confined to the limited and comparatively useless sphere of a slave; "and though," said he, "I must not be known to have spoken to you on this subject, yet if you will obtain Mr. Amos's consent to go to see your old master in Maryland, I will try and put you in a way by which I think you may succeed in buying yourself." He said this to me more than once; and as it was in harmony with all my aspirations and wishes, was flattering to my self-esteem, and could be attended with no harm that I could forsee, I soon resolved to make the attempt to get the necessary leave. Somewhat to my surprise, Master Amos made no objection; but gave me a pass to go to Maryland and back, with some remarks which showed his sense of the value of my services to him, and his opinion that I had earned such a privilege if I desired it. Furnished with this, and with a letter of recommendation from my Methodist friend to a brother preacher in Cincinnati, I started about the middle of September, 1828, for the east. By the aid of the good man to whom I had a letter, I had an opportunity of preaching in two or three of the pulpits in Cincinnati, when I took the opportunity of stating my purpose, and was liberally aided in it by contributions, made on the spot. My friend also procured some subscriptions in the city, so that in three or four days I left it with not less than one hundred and sixty dollars in my pocket. The annual Methodist Conference was about to be held at Chillicothe, to which my kind friend accompanied me, and by his influence and exertions I succeeded well there also. By his advice I then purchased a suit of respectable clothes, and an excellent horse, and travelled leisurely from town to town, preaching as I went, and, whereever circumstances were favorable, soliciting aid in my great object. I succeeded so well, that when I arrived at Montgomery county, I was master of two hundred and seventy-five dollars, besides my horse and my clothes. My master was surprised to see me dressed and mounted in so respectable a style, and I must say my horse was a good one, and my clothes better than Mr. R.'s; and he was a little puzzled to understand why I was so long in reaching home, for it was now Christmas, and he had been informed that I had left Kentucky in September. I gave him such an account of my preaching and getting the assistance of my friends, as, while it was consistent with the truth, and explained my appearance, did not betray to him my principal purpose. Amid expressions of an apparently cordial welcome, I could discern plainly enough the look of displeasure that a slave should have got possession of such luxuries; and he bantered me not a little, in his coarse way, upon my preaching, and my being so speedily converted into a "black gentleman." He asked for my pass, and saw that it was expressed so as to authorize my return to Kentucky. He then handed it to his wife, and desired her to put it into the desk. The maneuver was cool, but I resolved to maneuver too.

At night I was sent to such quarters as I had been accustomed to long enough,—the cabin used for a kitchen, with its earth floor, its filth, and its numerous occupants;—but it was so different from my accommodations in the free States for the last three months, and so incompatible with my nice wardrobe, that I looked round me with a sensation of disgust that was new to me; and instead of going to sleep, I sat down and deliberated upon the best plan to adopt for my next proceedings. I found my mother had died during my absence, and every tie which had ever connected me with this place was broken. Strangers were around me here, the slaves being those Mrs. R. had brought to her husband, and I had not a friend to consult but Master Frank, the brother of R.'s wife, before mentioned, who was now of age, and had established himself in business in Washington. To him I resolved to go, and as soon as I thought it time to start, I saddled my horse and rode up to the house. It was early in the morning, and my master had already gone to the tavern on his usual business, but Mrs. R. came out to look at my horse and equipments. "Where are you going, 'Siah?" was the natural question. I replied, "I am going to Washington, Mistress, to see Mr. Frank, and I must take my pass with me if you please." "O, everybody knows you here; you won't need your pass." "But I can't go to Washington without it. I may be met by some surly stranger, who will stop me and plague me, if he can't do any thing worse." "Well, I'll get it for you," she answered; and glad was I to have her give it to me, while she little imagined its importance to my plan.

My reception by Master Frank was all I expected, as kind and hearty as possible. He was delighted at my appearance, and I immediately told him all my plans and hopes. He entered cordially into them, with that sympathy which penetrates the heart of a slave, as little acustomed as I had been, to the exhibition of any such feeling on the part of a white man. I found he had a thorough detestation of Mr. R., whom he charged with having defrauded him of a large proportion of his property which he had held as guardian, though, as he was still on terms with him, he readily agreed to negotiate for my freedom, and bring him to the most favorable bargain. Accordingly, in a few days he rode over to the house, and had a long conversation with R. on the subject of my emancipation. He disclosed to him the facts that I had got some money and my pass, and urged that I was a smart fellow who was bent upon getting his freedom, and had served the family faithfully for many years; that I had really paid for myself a hundred times over, in the increased amount of produce I had raised by my skill and influence; and that if he did not take care, and accept a fair offer when I made it to him, he would find some day that I had the means to do without his help, and that he would see neither me nor my money; that with my horse and my pass I was pretty independent of him already, and he had better make up his mind to what was really inevitable, and do it with a good grace. By such arguments as these, Mr. Frank not only induced him to think of the thing, but before long brought him to an actual bargain, by which he agreed to give me my manumission papers for four hundred and fifty dollars, of which three hundred and fifty dollars were to be in cash, and the remainder in my note. My money and my horse enabled me to pay the cash at once, and thus my great hopes seemed in a fair way of being realized.

Some time was spent in the negotiations for this affair, and it was not till the 9th of March, 1829, that I received my manumission papers in due form of law. I was prepared to start immediately on my return to Kentucky, and on the 10th, as I was getting ready in the morning for my journey, my master accosted me in a very pleasant and friendly manner, and entered into conversation with me about my plans. He asked me what I was going to do with my freedom certificate; whether I was going to show it if I were questioned on the road. I told him yes, that I supposed it was given to me for that very purpose. "Ah," said he, "you do not understand the dangers to which you are exposed. You may meet with some ruffian slave-purchaser who will rob you of that piece of paper, and destroy it. You will then be thrown into prison, and sold for your jail fees, before any of your friends can know it. Why should you show it at all? You can go to Kentucky in perfect safety with your pass. Let me enclose that valuable document for you under cover to my brother, and nobody would dare to break a seal, for that is a State prison matter; and when you arrive in Kentucky you will have it all safe and sound." This seemed most friendly advice, and I felt very grateful for his kindness. I accordingly saw him enclose my precious piece of paper in two or three envelopes, seal it with three seals, and direct it to his Brother in Daviess county, Kentucky, in my care. Leaving immediately for Wheeling, to which place I was obliged to travel on foot, I there took boat, and in due time reached my destination. I was arrested repeatedly on the way, but by insisting always upon being carried before a magistrate, I succeeded in escaping all serious impediments by means of my pass, which was quite regular, and could not be set aside by any responsible authority.

It so happened that the boat which took me down from Louisville, landed me about dark, and my walk of five miles brought me to the plantation at bed-time. I went directly to my own cabin, where I found my wife and little ones well; and of course, we had a good deal to communicate to each other. Letters had reached the "great house," as the master's was always called, long before I had arrived, telling them what I had been doing, and the children of the family had been eager to communicate the great news to my wife, how I had been preaching, and raising money, and making a bargain for my freedom. It was not long before Charlotte began to tell me with much excitement what she had heard, and to question me about how I had raised the money I had paid, and how I expected to get the remainder of the thousand dollars I was to give for my freedom. I could scarcely believe my ears; but before telling her how the case exactly was, I questioned her again and again as to what she had heard. She persisted in repeating the same story as she had heard it from my master's letters, and I began to perceive the trick that had been played upon me, and to see the management by which Isaac R. had contrived that the only evidence of my freedom should be kept from every eye but that of his brother Amos, who was instructed to retain it till I had made up six hundred and fifty dollars, the balance I was reported to have agreed to pay. Indignation is a faint word to express my deep sense of such villainy. I was without a means of setting myself right. The only witness to the truth was my friend Frank, who was a thousand miles off; and I could neither write to him, nor get any one else to do it. Every man about me who could write was a slave-holder; and what chance had I to be believed, or to get evidence to the truth. In this dilemma I resolved not to deliver the paper to Amos, and told my wife I had not seen it since I was in Louisville. It might be in my bag, and perhaps it was lost; but at all events I did not wish to see it again at present; and if she should find it, and put it in some place which I did not know, it would be the best disposition of it. In a few minutes she went out, and I remained in ignorance where it was, till circumstances, presently to be mentioned, rendered it nec-essary for me to have it again.

The next morning I went up to the house, and showed myself to Mr. Amos, who welcomed me with apparent cordiali-ty, and who, I have no doubt, was really glad to see me, as my time and labor were important to him. We had a long conversa-tion, and after rallying me, as his brother had done, about my being turned fine gen-tleman, he entered upon the subject of my freedom, and told me what Isaac had writ-ten to him about the price I was to pay, how much I had already made up, &c. I found my wife was right. He then asked me

if I had not a paper for him. I told him I
certainly had received something for him,
of which I had taken the greatest care; but
that the last time I had seen it was at
Louisville, and that now it was not in my
bag, and I did not know what had become
of it. I could not conceive how it could be
lost, and yet I could not find it. He
expressed great concern, and sent me back
to the landing to see if it had been dropped
on the way. When the search proved in
vain, he told me that, after all, it was of no
consequence, for whenever I made up the
money, his brother would renew the paper.
"But," said he, "you have given too much
for yourself. Isaac has been too hard upon
you, and I don't see how you are going to
get so much in Kentucky."

All this was very smooth and pleasant
to a man who was in a frenzy of grief at the
base and apparently irremediable trick that
had been played upon him. I consoled
myself as well as I could, and set about my
work again, with as quiet a mind as I could
command, resolved to trust in God, and
never despair. Things went on as usual for
about a year, when, one day, Mr. Amos told
me that his brother kept writing to him
about his want of money; and intimated

that perhaps I might be ready to pay another instalment of my price. I told him I had nothing, as he knew very well, and that he never had said what he would allow me, or whether he would allow me anything for my labor in his service. That put an end to the conversation at the time, for he did not like the idea of paying for the labor I had bestowed on his farm, the care of his stock and his people. It was not long, however, before the subject was brought up again, and he said Isaac was perpetually telling him he must have money, and added that I must get ready to go to New Orleans with his son Amos, a young man of about twenty-one years of age, who was going down the river with a flat boat, and was nearly ready to start; in fact he was to leave the next day, and I must go and take care of him, and help him dispose of the cargo. The intimation was enough. Though it was not distinctly stated, yet I well knew what was intended, and my heart sunk within me at the near prospect of this fatal blight to all my long-cherished hopes. There was no alternative but death itself; and I thought that there was hope as long as there was life, and I would not despair even yet. The expectation of my fate, however, produced the degree of misery nearest to that of despair; and it is in vain for me to attempt to describe the wretchedness I experienced as I made ready to go on board the flat boat. I had little preparation to make, to be sure; and there was but one thing that seemed to me important. I asked my wife to sew up my manumission paper securely in a piece of cloth, and to sew that again round my person. I thought that having possession of it might be the means of saving me yet, and I would not neglect any thing that offered the smallest chance of escape from the frightful servitude that threatened me.

My wife and children accompanied me to the landing, where I bade them an adieu, which might be for life, and then stepped into the boat, which I found manned by three white men, who had been hired for the trip. Mr. Amos and myself were the only other persons on board. The load consisted of beef-cattle, pigs, poultry, corn, whiskey, and other articles from the farm, and from some of the neighboring estates, which were to be sold as we dropped down the river, wherever they could be disposed of to the greatest advantage. It was a common trading voyage to New Orleans, in which I was

embarked, the interest of which consisted
not in the incidents that occurred, not in
storms or shipwreck, or external disaster of
any sort; but in the storm of passions con-
tending within me, and the imminent risk of
the shipwreck of my soul, which was
impending over me nearly the whole period
of the voyage. One circumstance, only, I
will mention, illustrating, as other events of
my life have often done, the counsel of the
Saviour, "He that will be chief among you,
let him be your servant."

We were, of course, all bound to take
our trick at the helm in turn, sometimes
under the direction of the captain, and
sometimes on our own responsibility, as he
could not be always awake. In the daytime
there was less difficulty than at night,
when it required some one who knew the
river, to avoid sand-bars and snags, and
the captain was the only person on board
who had this knowledge. But whether day
or by night, as I was the only negro on the
boat, I was made to stand at least three
tricks to any other person's one; so that
from being much with the captain, and frequently thrown upon my own exertions, I
learnt the art of steering and managing the
boat far better than the rest. I watched the

maneuvers necessary to shoot by a sawyer, to land on a bank, or avoid a snag, or a steamboat, in the rapid current of the Mississippi, till I could do it as well as the captain. After a while the captain had a disease of the eyes, by which they became very much inflamed and swollen. He was soon rendered totally blind, and unable to perform his share of duty. This disorder is not an infrequent consequence of exposure to the intense light of the sun, doubled as it is by the reflection from the river. I was the person who could best take his place, and I was, in fact, master of the boat from that time till our arrival at New Orleans.

After the captain became blind, we were obliged to lie by at night, as none of the rest of us had been down the river before; and it was necessary to keep watch all night, to prevent depradations by the negroes on shore, who used frequently to attack such boats as ours, for the sake of the provisions on board. As I paced backwards and forwards on the deck, during my watch, it may well be believed I revolved many a painful and passionate thought. After all I had done for Isaac and Amos R., after all the regard they professed for me, and the value they could not

THE LIFE OF JOSIAH HENSON

but put upon me, such a return as this for my services, such an evidence of their utter inattention to my claims upon them, and the intense selfishness with which they were ready to sacrifice me, at any moment, to their supposed interest, turned my blood to gall and wormwood, and changed me from a lively, and I will say, a pleasant-tempered fellow, into a savage, morose, dangerous slave. I was going not at all as a lamb to the slaughter, but I felt myself becoming more ferocious every day; and as we approached the place where this iniquity was to be consummated, I became more and more agitated with an almost uncontrollable fury. I had met, on the passage, with some of my Maryland acquaintances who had been sold off to this region; and their haggard and wasted appearance told a piteous story of excessive labor and insufficient food. I said to myself, "If this is to be my lot, I cannot survive it long. I am not so young as these men, and if it has brought them to such a condition, it will soon kill me. I am to be taken by my masters and owners, who ought to be grateful friends, to a place and a condition where my life is to be shortened, as well as made more wretched. Why should I not prevent this wrong, if I can, by shortening their lives, or those of their agents in accomplishing such detestable injustice? I can do the last easily enough. They have no suspicion of me, and they are at this moment under my control, and in my power. There are many ways in which I can despatch them and escape, and I feel that I should be justified in availing myself of the first good opportunity." These were not thoughts which just flitted across my mind's eye, and then disappeared. They fashioned themselves into shapes which grew larger, and seemed firmer, every time they presented themselves; and at length my mind was made up to convert the phantom shadow into a positive reality. I resolved to kill my four companions, take what money there was in the boat, then to scuttle the craft, and escape to the north. It was a poor plan, maybe, and would very likely have failed; but it was as well contrived, under the circumstances, as the plans of murderers usually are; and blinded by passion, and stung to madness as I was, I could not see any difficulty about it. One dark, rainy night, within a few days of New Orleans, my hour seemed to have come. I was alone on deck; Mr. Amos and the hands were all asleep below, and I crept down noiselessly, got hold of an axe, entered the cabin, and looking by the aid of the dim light there for my victims, my eye fell upon Master Amos, who was nearest to me; my hand slid along the axe handle. I raised it to strike the fatal blow,—when suddenly the thought came to me, "What! commit murder! and you a Christian?" I had not called it murder before. It was self-defence,—it was preventing others from murdering me,—it was justifiable, it was even praiseworthy. But now, all at once, the truth burst upon me that it was a crime. I was going to kill a young man who had done nothing to injure me, but obey commands which he could not resist; I was about to lose the fruit of all my efforts at self-improvement, the character I had acquired, and the peace of mind which had never deserted me. All this came upon me instantly, and with a distinctness which made me almost think I heard it whispered in my ear; and I believe I even turned my head to listen. I shrunk back, laid down the axe, crept up on deck again, and thanked God, as I have done every day since, that I had not committed murder.

My feelings were still agitated, but they were changed. I was filled with shame and remorse for the design I had entertained, and with the fear that my companions would detect it in my face, or that a careless word would betray my guilty thoughts. I remained on deck all night, instead of rousing one of the men to relieve me, and nothing brought composure to my mind, but the solemn resolution I then made to resign myself to the will of God, and take with thankfulness, if I could, but with submission, at all events, whatever he might decide should be my lot. I reflected that if my life were reduced to a brief term, I should have less to suffer, and that it was better to die with a Christian's hope, and a quiet conscience, than to live with the incessant recollection of a crime that would destroy the value of life, and under the weight of a secret that would crush out the satisfaction that might be expected from freedom and every other blessing.

It was long before I recovered my self-control and serenity; but I believe no one but those to whom I have told the story myself, ever suspected me of having entertained such thoughts for a moment.

In a few days after this tremendous cri-

sis we arrived in New Orleans, and the little that remained of our cargo was soon
sold, the men were discharged, and nothing
was left but to dispose of me, and break up
the boat, and then Mr. Amos would take
passage on a steamboat, and go home.
There was no longer any disguise about the
purpose of selling me. Mr. Amos acknowledged that such were his instructions, and
he set about fulfilling them. Several
planters came to the boat to look at me;
and I was sent on some hasty errand, that
they might see how I could run. My points
were canvassed as those of a horse would
have been; and doubtless some account of
my human faculties was thrown into the
discussion of the bargain, that my value as
a domestic animal might be enhanced.
Amos had talked, with apparent kindness,
about getting me a good master, who
would employ me as a coachman, or a
house-servant; but as time passed on I
could discern no particular effort of the
kind. At length every thing was wound up
but this single affair. The boat was to be
sold, and I was to be sold, the next day, and
Amos was to set off on his return, at six
o'clock in the afternoon. I could not sleep
that night, which seemed long enough to

me, though it was one of the shortest in the
year. The slow way in which we had come
down had brought us to the long days and
the heat of June, and everybody knows
what the climate of New Orleans is at that
time of the year.

A little before daylight master Amos
awoke indisposed. His stomach was disor-
dered, but he lay down again, thinking it
would pass off. In a little while he was up
again and felt more sick than before, and it
was soon evident that the river fever was
upon him. He became rapidly worse, and
by eight o'clock in the morning he was
utterly prostrate; his head was on my lap,
and he was begging me to help him, to do
something for him, to save him. The tables
were turned. He was now rather more
dependent upon me than I had been upon
him the day before. He entreated me to
despatch matters, to sell the flat boat, in
which we two had been living by ourselves
for some days, and to get him and his
trunk, containing the proceeds of the trip,
on board the steamer as quick as possible,
and especially not to desert him so long as
he lived, nor to suffer his body, if he died,
to be thrown into the river. I attended to all
his requests, and by twelve o'clock that

day, he was in one of the cabins of the steamer appropriated to sick passengers.

All was done which could be done for the comfort and relief of anyone in such a desperate condition. But he was reduced to extremity. He ceased to grow worse after a day or two, and he must have speedily died, if he had not; but his strength was so entirely gone, that he could neither speak, nor move a limb; and could only indicate his wish for a teaspoonful of gruel, or something to moisten his throat, by a feeble motion of his lips. I nursed him carefully and constantly. Nothing else could have saved his life. It hung by a thread for a long time. We were as much as twelve days in reaching home, for the water was low at that season, particularly in the Ohio River; and when we arrived at our landing he was still unable to speak, and could only be moved on a sheet, or a litter. Something of this sort was soon fixed up at the landing, on which he could be carried to the house, which was five miles off; and I got a party of slaves belonging to the estate to form relays for the purpose. As we approached the house, the surprise at seeing me back again, and the perplexity to imagine what I was bringing along, with such a party, were extreme; but the discovery was soon made which explained the strange appearance; and the grief of father and mother, and brothers and sisters, made itself seen and heard. Loud and long were the lamentations over poor Amos; and when the family came a little to themselves, great were the commendations bestowed upon me, for my care of him and of the property.

We arrived home about the tenth of July, but it was not till the middle of August that Amos was well enough to move out of his chamber, though he had been convalescent all the while. As soon as he could speak, he told all I had done for him, and said, "If I had sold him, I should have died;" but it never seemed to occur to him or the rest of the family that they were under any, even the slightest, obligation to me on that account. I had done well as a slave, and to have it acknowledged, and to be praised for it, was compensation enough for me. My merits, whatever they were, instead of exciting sympathy, or any feeling of attachment to me, seemed only to enhance my money value to them. This was not the view I took of the case myself; and as soon as Amos began to recover, I began to meditate upon a plan of escape from the danger in which I constantly stood, of a repetition of the attempt to sell me in the highest market. Providence seemed to have interfered once to defeat the scheme, but I could not expect such extraordinary circumstances to be repeated, and I was bound to do every thing in my power to secure myself and my family from the wicked conspiracy of Isaac and Amos R. against my life, as well as against my natural rights in my own person, and those which I had acquired, under even the barbarous laws of slavery, by the money I had paid for myself. If Isaac would only have been honest enough to adhere to his own bargain, I would have adhered to mine, and paid him all I had promised. But his attempt to kidnap me again, after having pocketed three-fourths of my market value, absolved me from all obligation, in my opinion, to pay him any more, or to continue in a position which exposed me to his machinations. I determined to make my escape to Canada, about which I had heard something, as beyond the limits of the United States; for, notwithstanding there were free States in the Union, I felt that I should be safer under an entirely foreign jurisdiction. The slave States had their emissaries in the others, and I feared that I might fall into their hands, and need a stronger protection than might be afforded me by public opinion in the northern States at that time.

It was not without long thought on the subject that I devised a plan of escape; but when I had fully made up my mind, I communicated my intention to my wife, who was too much terrified by the dangers of the attempt to do any thing, at first, but endeavor to dissuade me from it, and try to make me contented with my condition as it was. In vain I explained to her the liability we were in of being separated from our children as well as from each other; and presented every argument which had weighed with my own mind, and had at last decided me. She had not gone through my trials, and female timidity overcame her sense of the evils she had experienced. I argued the matter with her, at various times, till I was satisfied that argument alone would not prevail; and then I said to her, very deliberately, that though it was a cruel thing for me to part with her, yet I would do it, and take all the children with

me but the youngest, rather than run the
risk of forcible separation from them all
and of a much worse captivity besides,
which we were constantly exposed to here.
She wept and entreated but found I was
resolute, and after a whole night spent in
talking over the matter I left her to go to
my work for the day. I had not gone far
when I heard her voice calling me. I waited
till she came up to me, and then, finding me
as determined as ever, she said, at last, she
would go with me It was an immense relief
to my nerves, and my tears flowed as fast
as hers had done before. I rode off with a
heart a good deal lighter.

She was living, at the time, near the
landing I have mentioned; for the plantation extended the whole five miles from the
house to the river, and there were several
different farms, all of which I was oversee-
ing, and, therefore, riding about from one
to another every day. The oldest boy was at
the house with Master Amos, the rest were
all with her. Her consent was given on
Thursday morning, and on the night of the
following Saturday, I had decided to set
out, as it would then be several days before
I should be missed, and I should get a good
start. Some time previously I had got my

wife to make me a large knapsack, big enough to hold the two smallest children; and I had arranged it that she should lead the second boy, while the oldest was stout enough to go by himself, and to help me carry the necessary food. I used to pack the little ones on my back, of an evening, after I had got through my day's work, and trot round the cabin with them, and go some little distance from it, in order to accustom both them and myself to the task before us.

At length the eventful night came. I went up to the house to ask leave to take Tom home with me that he might have his clothes mended. No objection was made, and I bade Master Amos "good night" for the last time. It was about the middle of September, and by nine o'clock in the evening all was ready. It was a dark, moonless night, and we got into the little skiff in which I had induced a fellow-slave to take us across the river. It was an agitating and solemn moment. The good fellow who was rowing us over, said this affair might end in his death; "but," said he, "you will not be brought back alive, will you?" "Not if I can help it," I answered. "And if you are overpowered and return," he asked, "will you conceal my part of the business?"

"That I will, so help me God," I replied.
"Then I am easy," he answered, "and wish
you success." We landed on the Indiana
shore, and I began to feel that I was my
own master. But in what circumstances of
fear and misery still! We were to travel by
night, and rest by day, in the woods and
bushes. We were thrown absolutely upon
our own poor and small resources, and
were to rely on our own strength alone.
The population was not so numerous as
now, nor so well disposed to the slave. We
dared look to no one for help. But my
courage was equal to the occasion, and we
trudged on cautiously and steadily, and as
fast as the darkness, and the feebleness of
my wife and boys would allow.

It was nearly a fortnight before we
reached Cincinnati; and a day or two previous to getting there, our provisions were
used up, and I had the misery to hear the
cry of hunger and exhaustion from those I
loved so dearly. It was necessary to run the
risk of exposure by daylight upon the road;
so I sprung upon it boldly from our hiding
place one morning, and turned towards the
south, to prevent the suspicion of my going
the other way. I approached the first house
I saw, and asked if they would sell we a lit-

tle bread and meat. No, they had nothing for black fellows. At the next I succeeded better, but had to make as good a bargain as I could, and that was not very successful, with a man who wanted to see how little he could give me for my quarter of a dollar. As soon as I had succeeded in making a purchase, I followed the road, still towards the south, till I got out of sight of the house, and then darted into the woods again, and returned northward, just out of sight of the road. The food which I bought, such as it was, put new life and strength into my wife and children when I got back to them again, and we at length arrived safe at Cincinnati. There we were kindly received and entertained for several days, my wife and little ones were refreshed, and then we were carried on our way thirty miles in a wagon.

We followed the same course as before, of travelling by night, and resting by day, till we arrived at the Scioto, where we had been told we should strike the military road of General Hull, in the last war with Great Britain, and might then safely travel by day. We found the road, accordingly, by the large sycamore and elm which marked its beginning, and entered upon it with

fresh spirits early in the day. Nobody had
told us that it was cut through the wilderness, and I had neglected to provide any
food, thinking we should soon come to
some habitation, where we could be supplied. But we travelled on all day without
seeing one, and laid down at night, hungry
and weary enough. I thought I heard the
howling of wolves, and the terror inspired
by this, and the exertions I used to keep
them off, by making as much noise as I
could, took away all power of sleeping, till
daylight, and rendered a little delay
inevitable. In the morning we were as hungry as ever, but had nothing to relieve our
appetites but a little piece of dried beef. I
divided some of this all round, and then
started for a second day's trip in the
wilderness. It was a hard trial, and this day
is a memorable one in my life. The road
was rough, of course, being neglected, and
the logs lying across it constantly; the
underbrush was somewhat cleared away,
and that was about all to mark the track.
As we went wearily on, I was a little ahead
of my wife and the boys, when I heard
them call to me, and, turning around, saw
that my wife had fallen over a log, and was
prostrate on the ground. "Mother's

dying," cried Tom; and when I reached her, it seemed really so. She had fainted. I did not know but it might be fatal, and was half distracted with the fear and the uncertainty. In a few minutes, however, she recovered sufficiently to take a few mouthfuls of beef, and this, with a little rest, revived her so much that she bravely set out once more.

We had not gone far, and I suppose it was about three o'clock in the afternoon, when we discerned some persons approaching us at no great distance. We were instantly on the alert, as we could hardly expect them to be friends. The advance of a few paces showed me they were Indians, with packs on their shoulders; and they were so near that if they were hostile, it would be useless to try to escape. So I walked on boldly, till we came close upon them. They were bent down with their burdens, and had not raised their eyes till now; and when they did so, and saw me coming towards them, they looked at me in a frightened sort of way for a moment, and then, setting up a peculiar howl, turned round, and ran as fast as they could. There were three or four of them, and what they were afraid of I could not imagine, unless they supposed I was the devil, whom they had perhaps heard of as black. But even then one would have thought my wife and children might have reassured them. However, there was no doubt they were well frightened, and we heard their wild and prolonged howl, as they ran, for a mile or more. My wife was alarmed, too, and thought they were merely running back to collect more of a party, and then to come and murder us, and she wanted to turn back. I told her they were numerous enough to do that, if they wanted to, without help; and that as for turning back, I had had quite too much of the road behind us, and that it would be a ridiculous thing that both parties should run away. If they were disposed to run, I would follow. We did follow on, and soon the noise was stopped; and as we advanced, we could discover Indians peeping at us from behind the trees, and dodging out of our sight, if they thought we were looking at them. Presently we came upon their wigwams, and saw a fine looking, stately Indian, with his arms folded, waiting for us to approach. He was apparently the chief, and saluting us civilly, he soon discovered that we were human beings, and spoke to his young men, who were scattered about, and made them come in, and give up their foolish fears. And now curiosity seemed to prevail. Each one wanted to touch the children, who were shy as partridges, with their long life in the woods; and as they shrunk away, and uttered a little cry of alarm, the Indian would jump back too, as if he thought they would bite him. However, a little while sufficed to make them understand what we were, and whither we were going, and what we needed; and as little, to set them about supplying our wants, feeding us bountifully, and giving us a comfortable wigwam for our night's rest. The next day we resumed our march, and found, from the Indians, that we were only about twenty-five miles from the lake. They sent some of their young men to point out the place where we were to turn off, and parted from us with as much kindness as possible.

In passing over the part of Ohio near the lake, where such an extensive plain is found, we came to a spot overflowed by a stream, across which the road passed. I forded it first, with the help of a sounding-pole, and then taking the children on my back, first, the two little ones, and then the others, one at a time, and lastly, my wife, I succeeded in getting them all safely across, where the ford was one hundred to one hundred and fifty yards wide, and the deepest part perhaps four feet deep. At this time the skin was worn from my back to an extent almost equal to the size of my knapsack.

One night more was passed in the woods, and in the course of the next forenoon we came out upon the wide plain, without trees, which lies south and west of Sandusky city. We saw the houses of the village, and kept away from them for the present, till I should have an opportunity to reconnoitre a little. When about a mile from the lake, I hid my companions in the bushes, and pushed forward. Before I had gone far, I observed on the left, on the opposite side from the town, something which looked like a house, between which and a vessel, a number of men were passing and repassing with activity. I promptly decided to approach them; and, as I drew near, I was hailed by one of the number, who asked me if I wanted to work. I told him yes; and it was scarcely a minute before I had hold of a bag of corn, which, like the rest, I emptied into the hold of the vessel lying at anchor a few rods off. I got into the line of laborers hurrying along the

plank next to the only coloured man I saw
engaged, and soon entered into conversation with him where they were going, the
best route to Canada, who was the captain, and other particulars interesting to
me, and communicated to him where I
came from, and whither I wished to go. He
told the captain, who called me one side,
and by his frank look and manner soon
induced me to acknowledge my condition
and purpose. I found I had not mistaken
him. He sympathized with me, at once,
most heartily; and offered to take me and
my family to Buffalo, whither they were
bound, and where they might arrive the
next evening, if the favorable wind continued, of which they were hurrying to take
advantage. Never did men work with a
better will, and soon two or three hundred
bushels were thrown on board, the hatches
were fastened down, the anchor raised,
and the sails hoisted. The captain had
agreed to send a boat for me, after sun-
down, rather than take me on board at the
landing; as there were Kentucky spies, he
said, on the watch for slaves, at Sandusky,
who might get a glimpse of me, if I brought
my party out of the bush by daylight. I
watched the vessel, as she left her moor-

ings, with intense interest, and began to fear that she would go without me, after all; she stretched off to so great a distance, as it seemed to me, before she rounded to. At length, however, I saw her come up to the wind, and lower a boat for the shore; and in a few minutes, my black friend and two sailors jumped out upon the beach. They went with me immediately, to bring my wife and children. But what was my alarm when I came back to the place where I had left them, to find they had gone! For a moment, my fears were overpowering; but I soon discerned them, in the fading twilight, at no great distance. My wife had been alarmed by my long absence, and thought I must have been discovered by some of our watchful enemies, and had given up all for lost. Her fears were not removed by seeing me returning with three other men; and she tried to hide herself. It was not without difficulty that I satisfied her all was right, for her agitation was so great that she could not, at once, understand what I said. However, this was soon over, and the kindness of my companions facilitated the matter very much. Before long, we were all on the way to the boat, and it did not require much time or labor to embark our luggage. A short row brought us to the vessel, and, to my astonishment, we were welcomed on board, with three hearty cheers; for the crew were as much pleased as the captain, with the help they were giving us to escape. A fine run brought us to Buffalo the next evening, but it was too late to cross the river that night. The next morning we dropped down to Black Rock, and the friendly captain, whose name I have gratefully remembered as Captain Burnham, put us on board the ferry-boat to Waterloo, paid the passage money, and gave me a dollar at parting. He was a Scotchman, and had done enough to win my enduring gratitude, to prove himself a kind and generous man, and to give me a pleasant association with his dialect and his country.

When I got on the Canada side, on the morning of the 28th of October, 1830, my first impulse was to throw myself on the ground, and giving way to the riotous exultation of my feelings, to execute sundry antics which excited the astonishment of those who were looking on. A gentleman of the neighborhood, Colonel Warren, who happened to be present, thought I was in a fit, and as he inquired what was the matter with the poor fellow, I jumped up and told him I was free. "O," said he, with a hearty laugh, "is that it? I never knew freedom make a man roll in the sand before." It is not much to be wondered at, that my certainty of being free was not quite a sober one at the first moment; and I hugged and kissed my wife and children all round, with a vivacity which made them laugh as well as myself. There was not much time to be lost, though, in frolic, even at this extraordinary moment. I was a stranger, in a strange land, and had to look about me at once, for refuge and resource. I found a lodging for the night; and the next morning set about exploring the interior for the means of support. I knew nothing about the country, or the people; but kept my eyes and ears open, and made such inquiries as opportunity afforded. I heard, in the course of the day, of a Mr. Hibbard, who lived some six or seven miles off, and who was a rich man, as riches were counted there, with a large farm, and several small tenements on it, which he was in the habit of letting to his laborers. To him I went, immediately, though the character given him by his neighbors was not, by any

means, unexceptionably good. But I
thought he was not probably any worse
than those I had been accustomed to serve,
and that I could get along with him, if honest and faithful work would satisfy him. In
the afternoon I found him, and soon struck
a bargain with him for employment. I
asked him if there was any house where he
would let me live. He said yes, and led the
way to an old two story sort of shanty, into
the lower story of which the pigs had broken, and had apparently made it their rest-
ing-place for some time. Still, it was a
house, and I forthwith expelled the pigs,
and set about cleaning it for the occupancy
of a better sort of tenants. With the aid of
hoe and shovel, hot water and a mop, I got
the floor into a tolerable condition by mid-
night, and only then did I rest from my
labor. The next day I brought the rest of
the Hensons to my house, and though
there was nothing there but bare walls and
floors, we were all in a state of great
delight, and my old woman laughed and
acknowledged that it was worth while, and
that it was better than a log-cabin with an
earth-floor. I begged some straw of Mr.
Hibbard, and confining it by logs in the
corners of the room, I made beds of it three

feet thick, upon which we reposed luxuri-
ously after our long fatigues.

Another trial awaited me which I had
not anticipated. In consequence of the great
exposures we had gone through, my wife
and all the children fell sick; and it was not
without extreme peril that they escaped
with their lives.

My employer soon found that my labor
was of more value to him than that of those
he was accustomed to hire; and I conse-
quently gained his favor, and his wife took
quite a fancy to mine, we soon procured
some of the comforts of life, while the nec-
essaries of food and fuel were abundant. I
remained with Mr. Hibbard three years,
sometimes working on shares, and sometimes for wages; and I managed in that
time to procure some pigs, a cow, and a
horse. Thus my condition gradually
improved, and I felt that my toils and sac-
rifices for freedom had not been in vain.
Nor were my labors for the improvement
of myself and others, in more important
things than food and clothing, without
effect. It so happened that one of my
Maryland friends arrived in the neighborhood, and hearing of my being here,
inquired if I ever preached now, and spread

the reputation I had acquired elsewhere, for my gifts in the pulpit. I had said nothing myself, and had not intended to say any thing, of my having ever officiated in that way. I went to meeting with others, when I had an opportunity, and enjoyed the quiet of the Sabbath when there was no assembly. I would not refuse to labor in this field, however, when desired to do so; and I hope it is no violation of modesty to state the fact that I was freqently called upon, not by blacks alone, but by all classes in my vicinity, the comparatively educated, as well as the lamentably ignorant, to speak to them on their duty, responsibility, and immorality, on their obligations to their Maker, their Saviour, and themselves.

It may, nay, I am aware it must, seem strange to many that a man so ignorant as myself, unable to read, and having heard so little as I had of religion, natural or revealed, should be able to preach acceptably to persons who had enjoyed greater advantages than myself. I can explain it, only by reference to our Saviour's comparison of the kingdom of heaven to a plant which may spring from a seed no bigger than a mustard-seed, and may yet reach such a size, that the birds of the air may take shelter therein. Religion is not so much knowledge, as wisdom;—and observation upon what passes without, and reflection upon what passes within a man's heart, will give him a larger growth in grace than is imagined by the devoted adherents of creeds, or the confident followers of Christ, who call him Lord, Lord, but do not the things which he says.

Mr. Hibbard was good enough to give my eldest boy, Tom, two quarters' schooling, to which the schoolmaster added more of his own kindness, so that my boy learned to read fluently and well. It was a great advantage, not only to him, but to me; for I used to get him to read much to me in the Bible, especially on Sunday mornings when I was going to preach; and I could easily commit to memory a few verses, or a chapter, from hearing him read it over. One beautiful summer Sabbath I rose early, and called him to come and read to me. "Where shall I read, father?" "Anywhere, my son," I answered, for I knew not how to direct him. He opened upon Psalm ciii. "Bless the Lord, O my soul, and all that is within me bless his holy name;" and as he read this beautiful outpouring of gratitude which I now first heard, my heart melted within me. I recalled, with all the rapidity of which thought is capable, the whole current of my life; and as I remembered the dangers and afflictions from which the Lord had delivered me, and compared my present condition with what it had been, not only my heart but my eyes overflowed, and I could neither check nor conceal the emotion which overpowered me. The words "Bless the Lord, O my soul" with which the Psalm begins and ends, were all I needed, or could use, to express the fulness of my thankful heart. When he had finished, Tom turned to me and asked, "Father, who was David?" He had observed my excitement, and added, "He writes pretty, don't he?" and then repeated his question. It was a question I was utterly unable to answer. I had never heard of David, but could not bear to acknowledge my ignorance to my own child. So I answered evasively, "He was a man of God, my son." "I suppose so," said he; "but I want to know something more about him. Where did he live? What did he do?" As he went on questioning me, I saw it was in vain to attempt to escape, and so I told him frankly I did not know. "Why, father," said he, "can't you read?" This was a worse question than the other, and if I had any pride in me at that moment, it took it all out of me pretty quick. It was a direct question, and must have a direct answer; so I told him at once I could not. "Why not," said he. "Because I never had an opportunity to learn, nor anybody to teach me." "Well, you can learn now, father." "No, my son, I am too old, and have not time enough. I must work all day, or you would not have enough to eat." "Then you might do it at night." "But still there is nobody to teach me. I can't afford to pay anybody for it, and of course no one can do it for nothing." "Why, father, I'll teach you. I can do it, I know. And then you'll know so much more, that you can talk better and preach better." The little fellow was so earnest, there was no resisting him; but it is hard to describe the conflicting feelings within me, at such a proposition from such a quarter. I was delighted with the conviction that my children would have advantages I had never enjoyed, but it was no slight mortification to think of being instructed by a child of twelve years old. Yet ambition, and a true desire to learn, for the good it would do my mind, conquered the shame, and I agreed to try. But I did not reach this state of mind instantly. I was greatly moved by the conversation I had had with Tom—so much so that I could not undertake to preach that day. The congregation were disappointed, and I passed the Sunday in solitary reflection in the woods. I was too much engrossed with the multitude of my thoughts within me to return home to dinner, and spent the whole day in secret meditation and prayer, trying to compose myself, and ascertain my true position. It was not difficult to see that my predicament was one of profound ignorance, and that I ought to use every opportunity of enlightening it. I began to take lessons of Tom, therefore, immediately, and followed it up, every evening, by the light of a pine knot, or some hickory bark, which was the only light I could afford. Weeks passed, and my progress was so slow that poor Tom was almost discouraged, and used to drop asleep, sometimes, and whine a little over my dullness, and talk to me very much as a schoolmaster talks to a stupid boy, till I began to be afraid that my age, my want of practice in looking at such little scratches, the daily fatigue, and the dim light, would be effectual preventives of my ever acquiring the art of reading. But Tom's perseverance and mine conquered at last, and in the course of the winter I did really learn to read a little. It was, and has been ever since, a great comfort to me to have made this acquisition; though it has made me comprehend better the terrible abyss of ignorance in which I had been plunged all my previous life. It made me also feel more deeply and bitterly the oppression under which I had toiled and groaned; but the crushing and cruel nature of which I had not appreciated, till I found out in some slight degree, from what I had been debarred. At the same time it made me more anxious than before to do something for the rescue and elevation of those who were suffering the same evils I had endured, and who did not know how degraded and ignorant they really were.

After about three years had passed, I improved my condition again by taking service with a gentleman by the name of Riseley, whose residence was only a few miles distant, and who was a man of more elevation of mind than Mr. Hibbard, and of superior abilities. At his place I began to reflect, more and more, upon the circumstances of the blacks, who were already somewhat numerous in this region. I was not the only one who had settled on the first spot in Canada which they had reached. Several hundreds of colored persons were in the neighborhood; and in the first joy of their deliverance, were going on in a way which, I could see, led to little or no progress in improvement. They were content to have the proceeds of their labor at their own command, and had not the ambition for, or the perception of what was within their easy reach, if they did but know it. They were generally working for hire upon the lands of others, and had not yet dreamed of becoming independent proprietors themselves. It soon became my great object to awaken them to a sense of the advantages which offered themselves to their grasp, and Mr. Riseley, seeing clearly the justness of my views, and willing to cooperate with me in the attempts to make them generally known among the blacks, permitted me to call meetings, at his house, of those who were known to be among the most intelligent and successful of our class. At these meetings we considered and discussed the subject, till we were all of one mind; and it was agreed, among the ten or twelve of us who assembled at them, that we would invest our earnings in land, and undertake the task, which, though no light one certainly, would yet soon reward us for our effort, of settling upon wild lands which we could call our own; and where every tree which we felled, and every bushel of corn we raised, would be for ourselves; in other words, where we could secure all the profits of our own labor.

The advantage of this course need not be dwelt upon in a country which is every day exemplifying it, and has done so for two hundred years and more; and has, by this very means, acquired an indestructible character for energy, enterprise, and self-reliance. It was precisely the Yankee spirit which I wished to instil into my fellow slaves, if possible; and I was not deterred from the task by the perception of the immense contrast in all the habits and character generated by long ages of freedom and servitude, activity and sloth, independence and subjection. My associates agreed with me, and we resolved to select some spot among the many offered to our choice, where we would colonize and raise our own crops, eat our own bread, and be, in short, our own masters. I was deputed to explore the country, and find a place to which I would be willing to migrate myself; and they all said they would go with me whenever such a one should be found. I set out accordingly in the autumn of 1834, and travelled on foot all over the extensive region between lakes Ontario, Erie, and Huron. When I came to the territory east of Lake St. Clair and Detroit River, I was strongly impresed with its fertility, its convenience, and, indeed, its superiority, for our purposes, to any other spot I had seen. I determined this should be the place; and so reported, on my return, to my future companions. They were wisely cautious, however, and sent me off again in the summer, that I might see it at the opposite seasons of the year, and be better able to judge of its advantages. I found no reason to change my opinion, but upon going further towards the head of Lake Erie, I discovered an extensive tract of government land, which, for some years, had been granted to a Mr. McCormick upon certain conditions, and which he had rented out to settlers upon such terms as he could obtain. This land being already cleared, offered some advantages for the immediate raising of crops, which were not to be overlooked by persons whose resources were so limited as ours; and we determined to go there first, for a time, and with the proceeds of what we could earn there, to make our purchases in Dawn afterwards. This plan was followed, and some dozen or more of us settled upon these lands the following spring, and accumulated something by the crops of wheat and tobacco we were able to raise.

I discovered, before long, that McCormick had not complied with the conditions of his grant, and was not, therefore, entitled to the rent he exacted from settlers. I was advised by Sir John Cockburn, to whom I applied on the subject, to appeal to the legislature for relief. We did so; and though McCormick was able, by the aid of his friends, to defeat us for one year, yet we succeeded the next, upon a second appeal, and were freed from rent, thereafter, so long as we remained. Still this was not our own land. The government, though it demanded no rent, might set up the land for sale at any time, and then we should, probably, be driven off by wealthier purchasers, with the entire loss of all our improvements, and with no retreat provided. It was manifest that it was altogether better for us to purchase before competition was invited; and we kept this fully in

mind during the time we stayed here. We
remained in this position six or seven
years; and all this while the colored population was increasing rapidly around us,
and spreading very fast into the interior
settlements and the large towns. The immi-
gration from the United States was incessant, and some, I am not unwilling to
admit, were brought hither with my
knowledge and connivance. I was glad to
help such of my old friends as had the spirit to make the attempt to free themselves;
and I made more than one trip, about this
time, to Maryland and Kentucky, with the
expectation, in which I was not disappointed, that some might be enabled to follow in my footsteps. I knew the route pretty well, and had much greater facilities for
travelling than when I came out of that
Egypt for the first time.

I did not find that our prosperity
increased with our numbers. The mere
delight the slave took in his freedom, rendered him, at first, contented with a lot far
inferior to that which he might have
attained. Then his ignorance led him to
make unprofitable bargains, and he would
often hire wild land on short terms, and
bind himself to clear a certain number of

acres; and by the time they were cleared and fitted for cultivation his lease was out, and his landlord would come in, and raise a splendid crop on the new land; and the tenant would, very likely, start again on just such another bargain, and be no better off at the end of ten years than he was at the beginning. Another way in which they lost the profits of their labor, was by raising nothing but tobacco, the high price of which was very tempting, and the cultivation of which was a monopoly in their hands, as no white man understood it, or could compete with them at all. The consequence was, however, that they had nothing but tobacco to sell; there was rather too much of it in the market, and the price of wheat rose, while their commodity was depressed; and they lost all they should have saved, in the profit they gave the trader for his corn and stores. I saw the effect of these things so clearly that I could not help trying to make my friends and neighbors see it too; and I set seriously about the business of lecturing upon the subject of crops, wages, and profits, as if I had been brought up to it. I insisted on the necessity of raising their own crops, saving their own wages, and securing the profits of their own labor, with such plain arguments as occurred to me, and were as clear to their comprehension as to mine. I did this very openly; and frequently, my audience consisted in part of the very traders whose inordinate profits upon individuals I was trying to diminish, but whose balance of profits would not be ultimately lessened, because they would have so many more persons to trade with who would be able to pay them a reasonable advance in cash, or its equivalent, on all their purchases. The purse is a tender part of the system; but I handled it so gently, that the sensible portion of my natural opponents were not, I believe, offended, while those whom I wished to benefit, saw, for the most part, the propriety of my advice, and took it. At least, there are now great numbers of settlers, in this region of Canada, who own their own farms, and are training up their children in true independence, and giving them a good elementary education, who had not taken a single step towards such a result before I began to talk to them.

I said none of the respectable traders were offended with me: but one man had the folly to arrest me for a small debt, under the pretense that I was about to leave the country, when I was only going to Detroit for a few days, in the spring, leaving my crops on the ground, and all my family at home but one little girl, who was to go to school for a few weeks. It was so absurd, however, that I was soon released by some of my friends, of whom I had many among the whites as well as the blacks.

While I remained at Colchester, I became acquainted with a Congregational missionary from Massachusetts, by the name of Hiram Wilson, who took an interest in our people, and was disposed to do what he could to promote the cause of improvement which I had so much at heart. He cooperated with me in many efforts, and I have been associated with him from 1836 to the present time. He has been a faithful friend and still continues his important labor of love in our behalf. Among other things which he did for us then, he wrote to a Quaker friend of his, an Englishman, by the name of James C. Fuller, residing at Skeneateles, New York, and endeavored to interest him in the welfare of our struggling population.

He succeeded so far, that Mr. Fuller, who was going on a visit to England, promised to do what he could among his friends there to induce them to aid us. He came back with fifteen hundred dollars which had been subscribed for our benefit. It was a great question how this sum, which sounded so vast to many of my brethren, should be appropriated. I had my own opinion pretty decidedly made up as to what it was best for us all to do with it. But in order to come to a satisfactory conclusion, the first thing to be done was to call a convention of delegates from every settlement of blacks that was within reach; that all might see that whatever was decided on, was sanctioned by the disinterested votes of those who were thought by their companions best able to judge what was expedient. Mr. Wilson and myself called a convention, therefore, to meet in London, Upper Canada, and it was held in June, 1838. I urged the appropriation of the money to the establishment of a manual-labor school, where our children could be taught those elements of knowledge which are usually the occupations of a grammar-school; and where the boys could be taught, in addition, the practice of some mechanic art, and the girls could be instructed in those domestic arts which are the proper occupation and ornament of their sex. Such an establishment would train up those who would afterwards instruct others; and we should thus gradually become independent of the white man for our intellectual progress, as we might be also for our physical property. It was the more necessary, as in many districts, owing to the insurmountable prejudices of the inhabitants, the children of the blacks were not allowed to share the advantages of the common school. There was some opposition to this plan in the convention; but in the course of the discussion, which continued for three days, it appeared so obviously for the advantage of all to husband this donation, so as to preserve it for a purpose of permanent utility, that the proposal was, at last, unanimously adopted, and a committee of three was appointed to select and purchase a site for the establishment. Mr. Wilson and myself were the active members of this committee, and after traversing the country for several months, we could find no place more suitable than that upon which I had had my eye for three or four years, for a permanent settlement, in the town of Dawn. We therefore bought two hundred acres of fine, rich land, on the river Sydenham, covered with a heavy growth of black walnut and white wood, at four dollars the acre. I had made a bargain for two hundred acres adjoining this lot, on my own account; and circumstances favored me so that the man of whom I purchased was glad to let me have them at a large discount from the price I had agreed to pay, if I would give him cash for the balance I owed him. I transferred a portion of the advantage of this bargain to the institution, by selling to it one hundred acres more, at the low price at which I had obtained them; and thus the school had three hundred acres of as fine land, and as well situated land, as Canada can show, at a very moderate cost. In 1842, I removed with my family to Dawn, and as a considerable number of my friends are there about me, and the school is permanently fixed there, the future importance of this settlement seems to be decided. There are many other settlements which are considerable; and indeed, the colored population is scattered over a territory, which does not fall short of three hundred miles in extent in each direction, and probably numbers not less than twenty thousand

persons in all. We look to the school, and
the possession of landed property by individuals, as two great means of elevation of
our oppressed and degraded race to a par-
ticipation in the blessings, as they have
hitherto been permitted to share only the
miseries and vices, of civilization.

My efforts to aid them, in every way in
my power, and to procure aid of others for
them, have been constant. I have made
many journeys into New York, Connect-
icut, Massachusetts, and Maine, in all of
which States I have found or made some
friends to the cause, and, I hope, some personal friends. I have received many liberal
gifts, and experienced much kindness of
treatment; but I must be allowed to allude
particularly to the donations received from
Boston, by which we have been enabled to
erect a sawmill, and thus to begin in good
earnest, the clearing of our lands, and to
secure a profitable return for the support of
our school, as among those which have
been most welcome and valuable to us.

I could give here a great many particulars, which would amuse and interest the
reader, if they did not instruct him. But it
is better not to indulge the inclination; and
I will conclude my narrative by simply

recording my gratitude, heartfelt and inexpressible, to God, and to many of my fellow-men, for the vast improvement in my condition, both physical and mental; for the great degree of comfort with which I am surrounded; for the good I have been enabled to effect; for the light which has risen upon me; for the religious privileges I enjoy, and the religious hopes I am permitted to cherish; for the prospects opening to my children, so different from what they might have been; and finally, for the cheering expectation of benefiting not only the present, but many future generations of my race.